PLAYSTRINGS

T0048144

THREE TUNES FROM SHAKESPEARE'S ENGLAND

arranged for
String Orchestra
by
NICHOLAS HARE

Sets of instrumental parts are available on sale (CH55341)
Each set contains:

4 Violin I
4 Violin II
4 Violin III
2 Viola I
2 Viola II
2 Cello I
2 Cello II
1 Double Bass

CHESTER MUSIC
(A division of Music Sales Limited)

PLAYSTRINGS

MUSIC FOR
STRING ORCHESTRA

PLAYSTRINGS provides an enjoyable and varied repertoire for young string orchestras, carefully structured in two levels which offer music suitable for players of two terms' to two years' and one years' to three years' experience.

The **Easy** level does not normally exceed Grade 2 in difficulty, while the **Moderately Easy** level includes some parts of around Grade 3 standard. Most of the parts are playable in first position only. **PLAYSTRINGS** is thus an ideal introduction to orchestral playing for young string players.

Allowing for occasional variations, the pieces have the following instrumentation:

EASY	**MODERATELY EASY**
Violin 1	Violin 1
Violin 2	Violin 2
Violin 3 *(=Viola 2)*	Violin 3
Viola 1 *(optional)*	Viola
Viola 2 *(optional, = Violin 3)*	Cello
Cello 1	Double Bass
Cello 2 *(optional)*	
Double Bass *(optional)*	

Scores are issued separately for each title, and a set of parts contains sufficient material for an orchestra of around 30 players. Larger groups will find that two or more sets of parts added together will cater adequately for their needs.

PLAYSTRINGS

MUSIQUE POUR ORCHESTRE A CORDES

PLAYSTRINGS offre un répertoire varié et intéressant aux jeunes exécutants des orchestres à cordes. Réparti avec soin en deux degrés de difficulté (**facile** et **moyenne force**), ce repertoire présente de la musique qui convient à des instrumentistes ayant deux trimestres à deux ans d'expérience, ou un an à trois ans d'expérience respectivement.

On peut jouer presque toutes les parties en première position. **PLAYSTRINGS** est donc une introduction idéale à l'exécution orchestrale pour les jeunes joueurs d'instruments à cordes.

A part quelques variations, les morceaux présentent l'instrumentation suivante:

FACILE	**MOYENNE FORCE**
Violon 1	Violon 1
Violon 2	Violon 2
Violon 3 *(= Alto 2)*	Violon 3
Alto 1 *(facultatif)*	Alto
Alto 2 *(facultatif, = Violon 3)*	Violoncelle
Violoncelle 1	Contrebasse
Violoncelle 2 *(facultatif)*	
Contrebasse *(facultatif)*	

Nous fournissons les partitions séparément pour chaque titre, et un matériel contient suffisamment de parties pour un orchestre de 30 exécutants environ. Deux matériels ou plus mis ensemble pourvoiront parfaitement aux besoins des groupes plus grands.

PLAYSTRINGS

MUSIK FÜR STREICHORCHESTER

PLAYSTRINGS bietet jungen Streichorchestern ein interessantes und abwechslungsreiches Programm, welches in zwei Schwierigkeitsgrade aufgeteilt wurde. Die einfacheren Musikstücke eignen sich für Spieler, deren Spielpraxis etwa zwischen einem halben Jahr und zwei Jahren liegt; die schwierigeren Stücke setzen eine Spielpraxis von etwa einem bis zu drei Jahren voraus.

Die Kategorie **"sehr leicht"** reicht im allgemeinen nicht über Schwierigkeitsgrad 2 hinaus, während einzelne Stimmen in der Kategorie **"leicht"** teilweise dem Schwierigkeitsgrad 3 entsprechen. Fast alle Stimmen werden nur in der 1. Lage gespielt. **PLAYSTRINGS** ist ideal zur Einführung junger Streicher in das Orchesterspiel.

Die Stücke sind mit geringen Ausnahmen wie folgt instrumentiert:

SEHR LEICHT	**LEICHT**
Violine 1	Violine 1
Violine 2	Violine 2
Violine 3 *(= Viola 2)*	Violine 3
Viola 1 *(ad libitum)*	Viola
Viola 2 *(ad lib., = Violine 3)*	Cello
Cello 1	Kontrabass
Cello 2	
Kontrabass *(ad lib.)*	

Zu jedem Titel ist eine Partitur lieferbar. Ein kompletter Stimmensatz zu jeder Partitur enthält Spielmaterial für etwa 30 Spieler. Bei grösseren Gruppen, können zwei oder mehr Stimmensätze verwendet werden.

THREE TUNES FROM SHAKESPEARE'S ENGLAND

arr. Nicholas Hare

1. GO FROM MY WINDOW

Variations

✱ N.B. There should be no break in rhythm between sections

CH55340

2

Var. IV

senza rit.

4

2. GREENSLEEVES

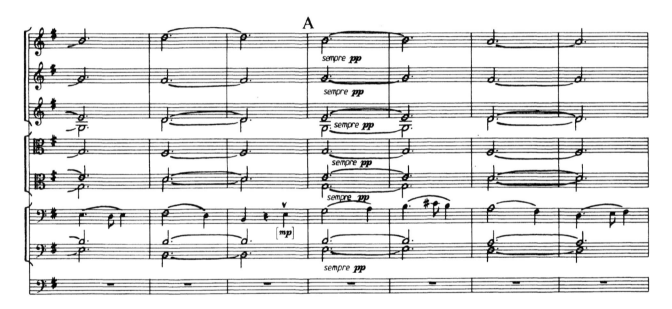

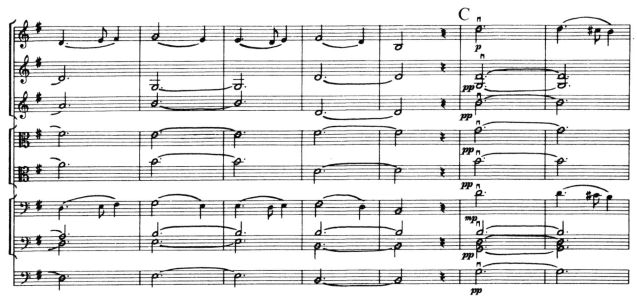

E

F

G

3. NOBODYES GIGGE